Rei

Owls
and Other Birds of Prey

Concept and Product Development: Editorial Options, Inc.
Series Designer: Karen Donica
Book Author: Mary E. Reid

**For information on other World Book
products, visit us at our Web site at
http://www.worldbook.com**

**For information on sales to schools and
libraries in the United States, call 1-800-975-3250.**

**For information on sales to schools and
libraries in Canada, call 1-800-837-5365.**

World Book, Inc.
233 N. Michigan Ave.
Chicago, Il 60601

Library of Congress Cataloging-in-Publication Data

Reid, Mary E.
    Owls and other birds of prey / [book author, Mary E. Reid].
        p. cm.—(World Book's animals of the world)
    Summary: Questions and answers explore the world of birds of prey, with an emphasis
on owls.
        ISBN 0-7166-1203-8 -- ISBN 0-7166-1200-3 (set)
        1. Owls—Juvenile literature. 2. Birds of prey—Juvenile literature. [I. Owls—Miscellanea.
2. Birds of prey—Miscellanea. 3. Questions and answers.] I. World Book, Inc. II. Title. III.
Series.
    QL696.S8 R45 2000
    598.9—dc21   00-021634

Printed in Singapore

1 2 3 4 5 6 7 8 9 05 04 03 02 01 00

World Book's Animals of the World

Owls
and Other Birds of Prey

Who-o-o gives a hoot?

World Book, Inc.
A Scott Fetzer Company
Chicago

Contents

Who is a flying monster?

Who is like
a helicopter?

Who rattles like
a snake?

Who might apply
for an office job?

What Is a Bird of Prey?

Owls are birds of prey. The prey are animals that the owls catch and eat. Other birds of prey include hawks, eagles, and falcons.

Like other birds of prey, owls have bodies that are especially well adapted for hunting and killing animals. Owls have powerful legs and feet. They also have sharp claws, or talons, that can pierce and grab small animals. Most owls have feathers on their legs and toes. The feathers protect them from cold—and from prey that might bite back!

Birds of prey have sharp, curved bills that are very strong. The upper and lower parts of the bill can work like powerful scissors to tear and cut meat. This barn owl probably crushed and broke the neck of its prey, killing it instantly. Owls swallow small prey whole.

Barn owl

Where in the World Do Owls Live?

There are more than 140 different kinds of owls. Owls live almost everywhere in the world where there is land, except Antarctica and some islands.

Grasslands are home to some kinds of owls. These owls include barn owls, great horned owls, and burrowing owls. Great horned owls, burrowing owls, and elf owls can also survive in the desert, where there is little or no rainfall.

Spotted owls live in forests of spruce or fir. Many owls live in different kinds of woodlands. The barred owl and the great gray owl live in hardwood forests. Northern hawk owls like the open woods.

One owl, the snowy owl, even lives on the frozen tundra. The tundra is a large, almost flat plain of the Arctic region. There are no trees in the tundra.

Grassland

Desert

Forest

Tundra

What Helps Owls Hunt at Night?

Owls are night-time hunters. Most owls have huge, staring eyes. They also have keen hearing. Their eyes and ears help them hunt at night.

In dim light, owls can see better than most other animals. The eyes of most owls have very large pupils. The pupil, or black part of the eye, is really an opening. An owl's pupil can open almost to the width of the whole eye. Thus, the pupil can take in every bit of light there is.

Most birds have eyes at each side of their head. They see a different scene with each eye. But an owl's eyes are at the front of its head. The owl sees the same scene with both eyes, just as a human does. An owl cannot move its eyes in their sockets, however. In order to see what is beside or behind it, the owl turns its whole head. Notice how far around this owl has turned its head to see what is behind.

Eagle owl

How Do Feathers Help Owls Hear?

Look at this owl's face. Those tufts of feathers that stick up like ears aren't ears at all! No one knows what they are for. An owl's large ear openings are at the sides of its head. The stiff feathers around the eyes act a lot like dish antennas. They reflect sound toward the ear openings.

Suppose an owl hears an animal sound. The sound is louder in one ear than in the other. This tells the owl that the animal is closer on that side. The owl turns its head until the sound is equally loud in both ears. Then it knows it is facing the animal.

An owl can also "hear" the height of a sound. It turns and tilts its head until it gets a perfect "fix" on where the sound is coming from. Owls eat mostly small animals that creep through grass and leaves on the ground. An owl's keen ears can hear the tiny sounds of prey—even when those sounds come from under snow!

Great horned owl

13

What Makes an Owl a Silent Hunter?

The night is dark. An owl hears exactly where a mouse is. It sees the mouse move in the grass. Suddenly the owl swoops silently down. It grabs the mouse with its talons.

How can the owl be so quiet? The soft, loose edges of the owl's flight feathers muffle the sound of its wings. Thus, the owl can silently sneak up on its prey. The flapping sounds made by most other birds of prey would have scared the mouse away!

Special effects, like time-lapse photography, can be used to show things in motion. This photo shows just one owl—in four different stages of flight. The flight of the owl is almost as silent as this photograph!

Owl in flight

15

What Do Owls Eat?

The favorite foods of North American owls are insects and rodents. Rodents are small animals such as mice, rats, shrews, and voles. Most owls stay in one place all year long, so they have to eat what they can find in each season. Owls also eat worms, frogs, lizards, smaller birds, and even larger animals such as rabbits and weasels. Some kinds of owls catch and eat fish. Owls can kill animals as large as they are or even larger.

When an owl lands on its prey, the owl hits the prey with its feet. If the prey is still alive, it breaks the animal's neck with a quick bite. Then it carries its prey up to a branch to eat.

Northern pygmy owl

What Are Owl Pellets?

When owls eat small prey, they usually swallow the animal whole. They tear larger prey into smaller pieces. However they eat, owls swallow many parts—bones, claws, fur, and feathers—that they cannot digest.

Juices in an owl's intestine dissolve and digest the usable parts of prey—the meat. Bones, claws, and other indigestible parts are squeezed into a hard pellet, which is spit up. An owl may spit up one pellet in the evening, before it goes hunting. Then, at night's end, the owl may spit up another pellet.

All birds of prey form pellets. People who study these birds take the pellets apart to learn what they eat. Here you see the contents of an owl pellet. Can you tell what the owl had for dinner?

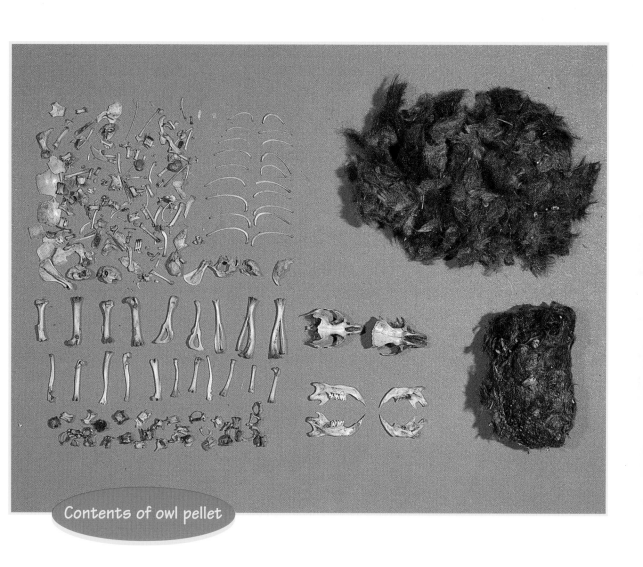

Contents of owl pellet

Who-o-o Is It?

It's not easy to spot an owl. But you may be able to hear one!

Different kinds of owls have many different calls. Some, like this great horned owl, seem to say "who-o-o, who-o-o" when they hoot. Others whistle, hiss, click, or chatter. One even makes a rasp that sounds like a rattlesnake. An owl hoots to claim its territory and to attract a mate. The word *owl* may in fact come from the hooting sound that the bird makes.

In the sign language of some Native American groups, the word for owl was formed with the hands. The sign is made by spreading fingers at each shoulder and flapping them. (This is the general sign for *bird.*) Then, to specify *owl,* the signer uses thumbs and index fingers to form two circles, which are put over the eyes. Try it, and see if a friend can guess who.

Great horned owl

How Do Owls Start a Family?

The owl you see nesting here is a great horned owl. Like most owls, it is not a nest-builder. She is using another bird's nest—which her mate found.

Great horned owls start their families in an interesting way. First, the male chooses a nesting place. Then he courts a female. He makes special calls, and he performs flying displays. He may offer the female a fresh mouse or other food. He may preen, or comb, her feathers with his beak.

After mating, a female owl usually lays three or four eggs. She sits on the nest and incubates, or warms, the eggs. On her belly, the female has a brood patch. This is a place where the skin is almost bare. It helps her body to warm the eggs directly.

While the female is sitting on the eggs, the male hunts. He finds food for both of them. In some kinds of owls, the male also has a brood patch. He helps keep the eggs warm.

Great horned owl
and owlet

How Do Owlets Grow?

When great horned owlets hatch, they are blind and have a thin coat of down—fine, soft feathers. The adult owls feed the owlets every 15 to 20 minutes all night long. Owl parents work very hard to feed themselves and their chicks!

Soon, the owlets have a heavier down coat. They grow strong and active. At 30 days, these owlets can hop about the nest and nearby branches. Gradually, their adult feathers appear. They will fledge, or be ready to fly, between 63 and 70 days after hatching.

Great horned owls bring small prey to the very young chicks. As the owlets grow, their parents offer bigger prey. The owlets quickly learn to tear this prey apart. They stay in the nesting area for several months. During this time, they learn to hunt for themselves, even though their parents continue to feed them.

Owlets

Where Can You Spot an Elf Owl?

This little bird, an elf owl, peers out from a hole in a saguaro *(suh GWAH roh)*. A saguaro is a giant cactus found in the southwestern United States and northwestern Mexico. The elf owl is one of the smallest owls in the world. It is only about 6 inches (15.2 centimeters) long.

An elf owl catches its food with its feet. It eats all kinds of insects, as well as mice, lizards, and spiders. The elf owl sits on a perch, watching. Then it darts out to catch a flying insect. Or, it flies around and scares an insect. Then it catches the insect as it jumps. When feeding owlets, this bird may make a trip a minute, catching and bringing insects to the nest!

Because they eat insects, elf owls are one of a very few kinds of owls that migrate. When winter comes to the United States, the elf owls living there fly south to Mexico. It is warmer in Mexico, so the elf owls there can still find plenty of insects to eat.

Elf owl

Who Lives in a Burrow?

Burrowing owls nest in underground tunnels. They often borrow homes from prairie dogs or ground squirrels. But if burrowing owls have to—and if the soil is easy to dig—they will use bills and feet to dig their own homes.

A male burrowing owl chooses a burrow and "decorates" it with grass. He performs courtship flights and sings to a female. After mating, the female lays eggs. She then incubates them in the dark nest chamber. The male owl feeds her. Later, both parents feed the chicks. If the owlets sense danger, they make rattling sounds. The rattling scares away such enemies as coyotes and foxes. These animals think the sounds are made by rattlesnakes.

Burrowing owls eat insects that they catch as they fly. They also eat mice, rats, and ground squirrels. They often hunt by sitting on a fence or other low perch to watch for prey.

Burrowing owls

Who Is White As Snow?

Snowy owls are as white as the snow in their home in the far north. These birds of prey live in northern Canada and Alaska, as well as in northern Europe and Asia. Because of their color and their silent flight, their prey may not see or hear them coming.

Snowy owls have especially thick feathers and extra body fat. The feathers and fat help these owls survive in very cold climates. In winter, when food is scarce, a snowy owl may go into a sleeplike state for up to 40 days. It uses very little energy. It needs no food. The owl becomes active again when the weather warms and food is available.

People welcome snowy owls because they kill rats, mice, and other rodents. This snowy owl has caught an Arctic hare almost as large as itself!

Snowy owl

What Makes a Hawk
a Bird of Prey?

Hawks are another kind of bird of prey. Hawks hunt during the day. So do most other birds of prey—except owls. (Most owls, as you know, hunt at night.) Like owls, hawks have strong legs and feet with sharp, curved talons. They also have powerful beaks for catching and eating prey.

This sharp-shinned hawk is a forest hawk. It has short, rounded wings and a long tail. This hawk can gain speed quickly and make sharp turns. These skills are important in hunting in woods where there are lots of trees.

A sharp-shinned hawk sits on a perch and watches for prey. Then it darts down and pounces. Its long, thin toes and sharp talons are just right for grasping songbirds, which it often catches in flight. This hawk has to eat 1/4 of its body weight each day. Its need for food keeps this bird busy hunting all day long!

Sharp-shinned hawk

How Do Hawks Care for Their Feathers?

Like all birds of prey, hawks spend time taking care of their flying equipment, which is their feathers. Hawks sometimes bathe by splashing at the edge of a lake or a stream. Or, they may take dust baths to get rid of fleas. This Cooper's hawk seems to be scratching an itch.

A bird's feathers are made of a network of straight, thin parts called barbs and parts with tiny hooks called barbules. The barbs and barbules can come apart and get ruffled. Birds smooth their feathers with their beaks. They put the barbs and barbules back together, like fixing a zipper. They spread oil on their feathers to protect and waterproof them. The oil comes from a small gland near the bird's tail.

Cooper's hawk

35

What Is a Buteo?

A buteo *(BYOO tee oh)* is a soaring hawk. A buteo glides high in the air, using its remarkable eyesight to scan the ground for prey. When a buteo like this red-tailed hawk spots prey, it dives down. It strikes the prey with sharp talons. Then it carries the prey to a perch, where the hawk can eat safely.

Buteos are powerful fliers. They need to be, because their prey include rabbits and pheasants. These animals are heavier than the prey eaten by forest hawks. It takes young buteos a long time to become good hunters.

When courting, male buteos do spectacular high flights and dives. A courting pair may hold claws and do cartwheels in the air.

Red-tailed hawk

Do Birds of Prey Migrate?

Birds of prey travel widely to get their food. Many of these birds also migrate from spring and summer breeding grounds in the north to warmer places where they can find food in winter.

One bird of prey that migrates is the Swainson's *(SWAYN suhnz)* hawk. It nests mainly on the prairies of the United States and Canada in North America. All summer, the Swainson's hawk eats mostly insects. When cold weather comes, the insects disappear. Flocks of Swainson's hawks then migrate up to 8,500 miles (13,600 kilometers) to the grasslands of Argentina in South America. There it is summer from December through March, and insects are plentiful.

Scientists learn about hawk migration by watching the birds. At migration time, bird watchers observe and count every hawk that flies over certain places.

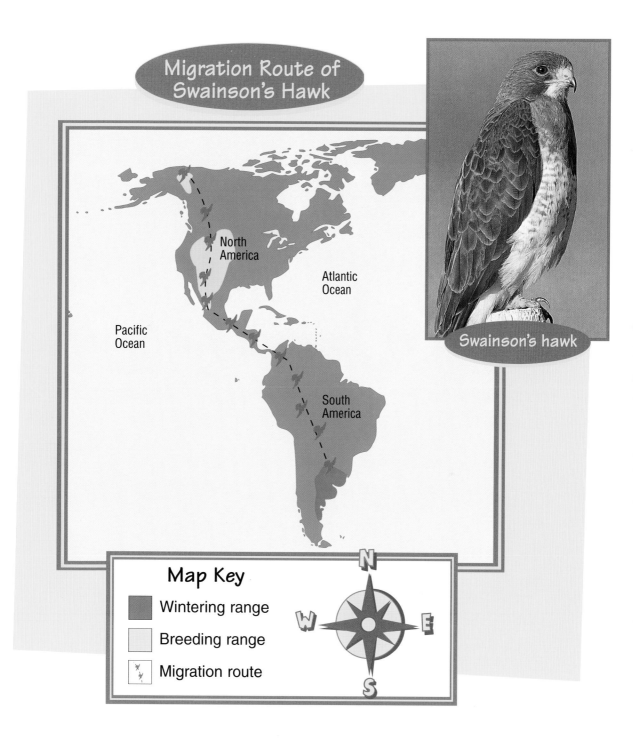

Migration Route of Swainson's Hawk

North America

Atlantic Ocean

Pacific Ocean

South America

Swainson's hawk

Map Key

Wintering range

Breeding range

Migration route

N
W E
S

What Are Kites?

Kites are slim birds that eat insects, tree frogs, lizards, and small mammals. Kites live on all continents except Antarctica. In the United States, kites are found in Florida and other southern states.

This snail kite catches its food while flying. It snatches up dragonflies and other large insects with its claws. Or, it zooms past a tree and grabs a lizard or a frog from a branch. The kite also drinks while in flight. It flies down low over the water to sip.

Kites also do some of their nest-building tasks "on the wing." Kites use twigs to build their nests. To gather the twigs, they fly over the treetops. They break off small branches while they are still in flight.

Snail kite

How Did the Secretary-Bird Get Its Name?

Long ago, secretaries wrote and copied letters by hand. They stuck quill pens behind their ears when they weren't using them. Look at the birds in this picture. Their black plumes reminded people of quill pens. So they named the bird the secretary-bird.

Secretary-birds live on grassy plains in parts of Africa. These birds are tall, and they have much longer legs than other birds of prey. They run through the grass, attacking prey with their feet and wings. Secretary-birds catch and eat large insects, snakes, small mammals, and lizards. They also eat the eggs of other birds.

When it's time to nest, secretary-birds build unusual homes. They use sticks, leaves, and grass to make a kind of platform. Both parents incubate the eggs and share in feeding the chicks.

Secretary-birds

Which Bird of Prey Flies the Fastest?

A peregrine *(PEHR uh grihn)* falcon can fly faster than almost every other kind of bird. In a dive with its wings folded, it can go more than 200 miles (320 kilometers) per hour. When it is flapping its wings and flying straight, it can go as fast as 60 miles (97 kilometers) per hour.

Peregrine falcons were once the most widespread daytime birds of prey in the world. This may be because they are such good hunters. Their main prey are live birds, such as pigeons, ducks, and other water birds. A falcon perches in a high place or circles in the air. When it spots prey, the falcon makes a spectacular dive. It grabs the prey in midair with its talons.

Peregrine falcon

45

Is Flapping the Only Way to Fly?

The bird of prey you see here is a kestrel *(KEHS truhl)*. It can hover, or stay in one place in the air, with its wings beating rapidly. For this reason, the kestrel is known as a windhover.

As it hovers, a kestrel also hunts for prey. It dives down and uses its strong talons to strike its prey. Its catch might be a mouse, a lizard, or a grasshopper.

Kestrels live all over the world, except Antarctica. They nest in trees or on cliffs or tall buildings. While looking for prey, kestrels may perch on telephone wires or poles. Kestrels can often be seen along country roads. They can be spotted around suburban houses, too.

Kestrel

Can Birds Help Predict the Weather?

Not really! But the people who lived in ancient Greece thought ospreys *(AHS preez)* did control the weather. These huge birds were supposed to be able to stir up violent winds and cause bad storms. More recently, some North Americans who fished for a living also watched for ospreys. An osprey in flight was thought to be a sign that a storm was brewing.

The osprey is a great fishing bird. It has an amazing wingspan of up to 6 feet (1.8 meters). As it soars over water, the bird watches for prey—mostly fish. Then it dives down and snatches up a fish with its talons. Tiny spines on its feet help the bird grip the slippery fish.

Ospreys make big nests of sticks in dead trees or on power poles. Osprey chicks have camouflage coloring. This may be because their nests are so visible. Bald eagles, crows, and ravens will eat osprey chicks—if they can find them.

Osprey

What Do Vultures Eat?

Vultures do not hunt live animals. Instead, they feed on carrion. Carrion is the meat of an animal that is already dead.

Vultures do not eat rotten meat. They prefer it freshly killed. Some vultures, like these turkey vultures, find carrion by smell. Others, such as black vultures, don't have such a fine sense of smell. They follow the turkey vultures to find food. They tear the meat apart with their beaks and talons. Then they eat it.

Unlike other birds of prey, vultures do not have powerful feet. Perhaps this is because they don't need to use their feet to catch and kill prey. Their heads and necks are bare, with no feathers.

Vultures are important because they help clean up the environment. They eat dead animals before the rotting bodies can become a source of disease.

Turkey vultures

Is the California Condor Really a Vulture?

Yes, the California condor is a member of the vulture family. Like other vultures, it has weak feet, and its head and neck are bare. But this vulture does have keen eyesight, and it is a powerful flyer. A California condor can soar and glide a long way.

The California condor is in danger of becoming extinct. A big problem is loss of habitat. Condors need huge areas of open country where elk, cattle, and deer live. Condors feed on the carrion of these large animals. As cities grow, these animals have less and less land on which to live. Without their prey, the condors cannot survive either.

Fortunately, there is a recovery plan for these condors. They are being bred in animal centers in California and Idaho. The plan is to reintroduce condors into the wild in two different places. It is hoped that this will give the birds a good chance to survive.

California condor

Is There Just One Family of Eagles?

Different kinds of eagles actually belong to different families. The bald eagle is a member of the fish-eagle family. The golden eagle is more closely related to buteos, or soaring hawks.

This harpy eagle of the South American rain forests is one of the biggest and strongest eagles in the world. Harpy eagles weigh more than 10 pounds (4.5 kilograms). When they spread their wings, their wingspan measures 7 feet (2 meters). A harpy eagle can kill an animal as heavy as a sloth or a monkey.

Harpy eagles are named after the "flying monsters" that appear in the myths of ancient Greece and Rome. There are eagles in the myths of many different groups of people, including the Native Americans. Perhaps this is because eagles are among the largest and most powerful birds of prey.

Harpy eagle

Which Eagle Is a Pirate?

Bald eagles are well known for pirating, or stealing, fish from other fishing birds. Two biologists once saw an eagle attack an osprey that was carrying a fish high in the air. The eagle fought until the osprey dropped the fish. Then the eagle dived and caught the falling fish before it hit the water.

Bald eagles also eat water birds, such as coots and herons. Sometimes they eat carrion. Bald eagles are even big and strong enough to kill and eat geese and jackrabbits.

Eagles build big, stick nests called aeries *(AIR eez)* in tall treetops or on cliffs. Eagles often use the same aerie year after year, adding new sticks each year. Young bald eagles have dark feathers all over. They don't get their white head feathers until they are 6 or 7 years old. By then, they are skilled hunters and are old enough to breed.

Bald eagle

Which Bird of Prey
Is a Runner?

The bird you see here is a roadrunner. Some people consider roadrunners to be birds of prey. Roadrunners can fly, but they seldom do. They are most at home on the ground. They can run 15 miles (24 kilometers) an hour.

For a bird, however, the roadrunner's legs are fairly long. They are also very sturdy. Roadrunners chase down their prey, which include insects, gophers, mice, lizards, baby birds, and snakes. Roadrunners usually swallow their prey whole—after killing it, of course. They kill larger prey by whacking it against a rock—or something else that's hard.

Roadrunners live in the deserts of southwestern United States and Mexico. You can probably guess how they got their name. These comical birds often run down roads in front of moving cars. Then, when the cars get too close, they dart off into the desert brush.

Roadrunner

Are Birds of Prey in Danger?

In the United States and Mexico, the California condor is an endangered species. Here you see a baby condor that is being raised in a zoo. At the right is a condor hand puppet, which is being moved by a zoo worker. The baby thinks it is a real condor—maybe even its mother. The puppet helps the chick get used to being around condors.

In other parts of the world, some hawks, falcons, and kestrels are also endangered. Harpy eagles are rare—and are in danger of becoming extinct. The Spanish imperial eagle is on the list of endangered animals.

Owls, hawks, and other birds of prey need places to nest. They also need wide areas in which to hunt for prey. Unfortunately, many birds of prey are losing their homes. Their natural habitats are being destroyed. Conservationists are working to protect those habitats. They are also setting aside nature preserves, where the birds can live in safety.

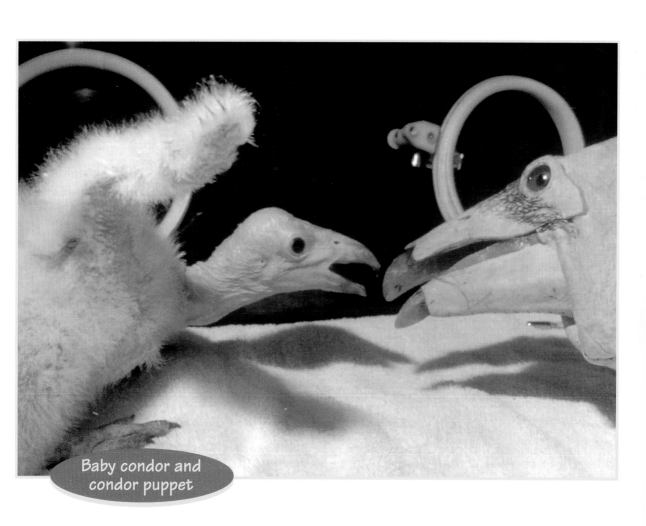

Baby condor and
condor puppet

Bird of Prey Fun Facts

→ When an elf owl is in danger, it may play dead—just like an opossum.

→ The male peregrine falcon bows to the female before mating.

→ Barn owls are sometimes called monkey-faced owls because their heart-shaped faces, beady eyes, and funny ways are like a monkey's.

→ Some owls build nests in old holes made by woodpeckers. These holes may be in trees or in cacti.

→ Owls can turn their heads almost completely upside-down to see what is above them.

→ The feathers of snowy owls are as warm as the thickest furs of other animals that live in cold places.

→ Groups of migrating hawks are called kettles. Kettles use upward movements of air to help them fly high.

→ How does an osprey grip a large fish? With both feet! The feet are placed one behind the other. The fish faces forward.

Glossary

aerie A nest built on a cliff or other high place.

beak A bird's bill that is hooked.

bill The hard part of a bird's jaws.

birds of prey Birds that hunt animals for food.

breeding ground A place to give birth.

camouflage coloring Coloring that hides an animal.

claws An animal's feet with sharp, hooked nails.

courts Tries to please for mating.

darts Moves suddenly and quickly.

digest To change food so that an animal's body can use it.

down Soft feathers.

energy The power to do things.

extinct Dead and not alive again.

fledge To grow feathers for flying.

flight Movement with wings in air.

flocks Groups of animals that stay together, especially birds.

habitat An animal's home.

incubate To sit on eggs to make them warm enough to hatch.

migrate To move from one region to another, especially at a particular time of year.

muffle To stop or soften a sound.

pellet A small ball of food that can't be digested and is spit up.

perch The place where a bird sits.

pierce To go into or through.

prey Animals that other animals eat.

reflect To give back sound or light.

ruffled Not smooth.

spines Stiff, pointed parts.

survive To keep on living.

talons Claws.

vole An animal related to rats.

waterproof Keeping water out.

wingspan The distance between the tips of a bird's wings when fully extended.

Index

(**Boldface** indicates a photo, map, or illustration.)

Picture Acknowledgments: Front & Back Cover: © C. K. Lorenz, Photo Researchers; © Tom Branch, Photo Researchers; © Barbara Gerlach, Tom Stack & Associates; © Roger Wilmhurst, Photo Researchers.
AP/Wide World Photos 61; © Tom Brakefield, Bruce Coleman Inc. 45; © Tom Branch, Photo Researchers 9; © J. A. L. Cooke, Animals Animals 59; © Alan & Sandy Carey, Photo Researchers 57; © Stephen Dalton, Photo Researchers 5, 7, 15, 47; © Phil A. Dotson, Photo Researchers 31; © Kenneth W. Fink, Photo Researchers 53; © Barbara Gerlach, Tom Stack & Associates 39; © John Gerlach, Tom Stack & Associates 5, 43, 51; © Michael Giannechin, Photo Researchers 23; © Ted Levin, Animals Animals 41; © C. K. Lorenz, Photo Researchers 3, 5, 9, 21, 27, 29; © Anthony Mercieca, Photo Researchers 4, 17, 55; © S. Nielsen, Bruce Coleman Inc. 33; © Hans Reinhard, Bruce Coleman Inc. 9; © Laura Riley, Bruce Coleman Inc. 37; © Len Rue, Jr., Photo Researchers 11; © Tom & Therisa Stack, Tom Stack & Associates, 49; © Lynn M. Stone, Bruce Coleman Inc. 13; © Kim Taylor, Bruce Coleman Inc. 35; © Greg Vaughn, Tom Stack & Associates 9; © Roger Wilmhurst, Photo Researchers 25; © Jim Zipp, Photo Researchers 19.
Illustrations: WORLD BOOK illustration by Michael DiGiorgio 36; WORLD BOOK illustration by Karen Donica 39.